AWAKENING THE

AFRICAN CONSCIOUSNESS

BY: MELVIN ORANGE JR.

Contents

Introduction 1

Chapter 1: The Motherland 7

Chapter 2: The Great Ancient African Egyptians 15

Chapter 3: We Are Human Beings 33

Chapter 4: Living in Two Worlds 43

Chapter 5: Time and Space 49

Chapter 6: Consciousness 55

Chapter 7: Reality 61

Chapter 8: Fearlessness 67

Chapter 9: Free Will 71

Chapter 10: Morals 75

Chapter 11: Good vs. Evil 79

Chapter 12: Power 85

Chapter 13: Pain 89

Chapter 14: Anger 93

Chapter 15: Happiness 97

Chapter 16: Life and Death 101

Chapter 17: Awaken 105

The Self-Enlightened 109

Introduction

"The best thing a man can be is sincere."

– Malcom X

What exactly does it mean to be sincere? Being extremely kind and friendly does not make you sincere. To be sincere you must be free from deceit, clean and pure. To be sincere is to tell the truth, saying what you genuinely believe. Before becoming genuine, to be sincere, you must become aware of who you are, your true, permanent and eternal identity. This book is filled with truth, sincerity and authenticity. It is hard to find real sincerity from people nowadays, it is just a faked-up attitude most of the time.

Most people don't tell the truth, saying what they genuinely believe, they do just the opposite. The opposite of sincerity is bullshit, and bullshit is everywhere. The world is filled with people who deceive and bullshit just to get their way, to get over or to get rich. You can find bullshit much faster than you can find sincerity in this world. The amount of bullshit in the world now is enormous, it surrounds us, and we don't see it for what it is. What exactly is Bullshit? Bullshit is the attempt to purposely mislead and the attempt to impress. Each one of us have

Introduction

contributed our own share of bullshit but bullshit extends beyond individuals to organizations and governments.

The purpose of this book is to awaken your consciousness, free your mind from the bullshit and give you the ability to identify bullshit. This book will also help you avoid being deceived by bullshit and to give your own intuition the ability to recognize the circle of truth. This book is short and straight to the point, the goal is to lead you to self-enlightenment, but self-enlightenment is ultimately up to you to figure out and obtain on your own. Read this book with an open, pure and thoughtful mind set as you would the Bible, Quran or any important spiritual text.

You will find things that you can cherish forever in this book like absolute truths, knowledge and wisdom, so take your time, think carefully and read through this book thoroughly. We are thinking human beings whether the information is right or wrong. This book will turn you in the right direction or confirm that you are walking in the right direction towards truth, you can be certain everything in this book is true, study and believe in it. There is much to learn in this rather small book, understand language is about meaning not

Introduction

amount of words, I am precise in my use of words because thoughts and ideas can only have meaning if they can be expressed and understood naturally. The ones who are psychologically and spiritually in balance and the ones who have knowledge of absolute truths, knowledge and wisdom, have a job, to serve and teach the ones who lack these qualities. Ignorance is defined as lack of knowledge. The less knowledge you have, the less awaken your consciousness is and the more knowledge you have, the more awaken your consciousness is. The less awakened man is easily deceived. "Without education, people will accept anything. Without education, people don't know why they are doing what they are doing." – Fred Hampton

CHAPTER 1

The Motherland

Where was the first human being born? The first human being was born in Africa. The name Africa is of African origin. The word Africa comes from the Egyptian word "Afru-ika" meaning "Motherland". The term Motherland is still used in reference to Africa today. The Great Ancient African Egyptians named Africa the Motherland because Africa is where all human life began. Mankind was born in South Africa, everyone in the world has African influences, that includes Ancient Greece and Ancient Rome.

For example, the Latin and the Greek have African Egyptian language Influences. The Latin used the word "Aprica" meaning "sunny." The Greek used the word "Aphrike" meaning "without cold." The name Africa came from the Romans, in western use. "Africanus" is from the Latin and "Afru-ika" is from the African Egyptians and the name "Afru-ika" was around and in existence long before the name "Africanus." The Ancient Romans and the Ancient Greeks spent time in Northern Africa. The time the Romans were in Northern Africa was around the 300s BC. to around the 400s AD. The time the Greeks were in Northern

The Motherland

Africa was around the 300s BC. to around the 200s AD. The European culture does not begin to take off and make their mark until after these first civilized Europeans entered Northern Africa. Africa is the motherland for everything and that includes knowledge and wisdom.

There are many significant things about Africa, the Motherland, it is the greatest and most unique continent in the world. Africa is the second largest continent, the first is Asia. Africa is the only continent to stretch from the Northern Temperate Zone to Southern Temperate Zone, Africa straddles the equator. Africa is surrounded by the Mediterranean Sea to the north, the Red Sea along the Sinai Peninsula to the northeast, the Indian Ocean to the southeast and the Atlantic Ocean to the west. One of the largest freshwater lakes in the world is in Africa, Africa's Lake Victoria.

The largest land animal in the world lives in Africa, the African Elephant.

The tallest land animal in the world lives in Africa, the African Giraffe.

The world's largest bird lives in Africa, the African Ostrich.

The Motherland

The fastest land animal in the world lives in Africa, the African cheetah.

The world's largest reptile lives in Africa, the African Nile Crocodile.

The world's largest primate lives in Africa, the African Gorilla.

The world's most ferocious animal lives in Africa, the African Lion.

Africa, the motherland is rich in itself. Africa has the largest reserves of precious metals with over half of the gold reserves, over more than half of the cobalt reserves and almost all the platinum reserves. Africa has almost half of the earths mineral resources and is one of the largest oil exporters in the world.

Africa is the hottest continent in the world. The Kalahari Desert, the Namib Desert, the Sahara Desert and Drylands cover about 70% of land surface area. The Sahara Desert is the largest desert in the world and is larger than the continental USA.

The Motherland

The Great Ancient African Egyptians believed that they were the Sons and Daughters of the Sun and there are still some African Egyptians today that still believe it. A few reasons why the Great Ancient African Egyptians believed Africans were the Sons and Daughters of the Sun is because they are from the hottest continent in the world and Africans have the most, Melanin, we are the darkest people on the planet.

Melanin protects Africans from the Sun and is responsible for the pigmentation in the Africans skin. Melanin is a neurochemical that is produced in part of the pituitary gland, in the brain. Melanin in found in everything, from water, to land, to the forming of the nervous system. Only people of color have access to this form of energy. Africa, The Motherland is the greatest continent in the world and it is not only responsible for the birthplace of mankind, knowledge and wisdom but is also responsible for the world's first, greatest and longest lasting civilization ever in the world, The Great Ancient African Egyptian Civilization.

CHAPTER 2

The Great Ancient African Egyptians

The world's first and greatest civilization emerged around 3100 BC. The Great Ancient African Egyptians did many significant things from the Great Pyramids of the Old Kingdom, to the military conquest of the New Kingdom, to the religious beliefs that help shape the concept and development of religion around the world. The Ancient African Egyptians were mystics and considered themselves to be Gods of the earth, and they were. Human beings originated in Africa, and the African Egyptians civilization is the first, and greatest civilization ever. Africans, African Americans, anyone with African descent in them, should be proud to be a direct descendant of the God's of the earth, the Ancient African Egyptians. The reason why the Ancient African Egyptians are the God's of the earth is because they come directly from the first African human beings to walk the earth.

The Ancient African Egyptians were the greatest and left behind evidence of themselves all over the world, from the African Egyptian writings known as hieroglyphics, to the Pyramids, and are known as the world's most advanced civilization. The Ancient African Egyptians understood advanced mathematics and built some of the world's largest monuments, in size, without modern technology, that's amazing. The Ancient African Egyptians were the Gods of the earth, they precisely, excellently and perfectly built the Great Pyramid of Giza in the geographical center of the earth's landmass, directly in the middle of the earth, perfectly aligned with the lines of latitude and longitude. It is extremely accurate, perfectly aligned towards the north and aligned pointing to the star constellation

Orion's Belt. That is incredible, if that's not godly, I don't know what is.

To understand the Ancient African Egyptian Gods, you must understand where they come from. They come from the first human beings to ever walk the earth. Mankind was born in South Africa and not only did these first Africans survive, they thrived and created the greatest civilization known to man.

The first human beings were African and were small in number and could have easily become extinct, but the first African human beings were smart, unique and strong, they transformed themselves into the best hunters on the planet. The first African human beings were always in danger, they went out onto the grasslands of South Africa to hunt and gather meats, fruits, plants, nuts, seeds, any source of food, where they could have easily become prey to four legged predators. These first, original Ancient Africans were genius, they learned and recognized over thousands of plants and all their vegetation stages, roots leaves and fruits. The first African human beings were smart enough to understand and distinguish what was edible and inedible and find substances to heal different illnesses.

The first human beings, the Africans followed the Nile River from South Africa up to North Africa. The Nile River is the only river in the world that flows from south to north, instead of north to south, that's outstanding. The Nile River has two branches, the Blue Nile which originates in Ethiopia and the White Nile which originates in Kenya, Uganda, and the Tanzania area, these are the places where the first human beings were born. The first human beings, the Africans, followed the Nile River to the north to northern Africa, to Egypt and created the best civilization known to man, the Great African Egyptian Pharaonic Civilization.

The Ancient African Egyptians story of creation is the story of Osiris, Isis, and Horus. The name Osiris is the Latinized version of the African Egyptian "Usir", which means "mighty or powerful"; and Isis is the Greek version of the African Egyptian "Aset", which means "female or queen of the throne"; and Horus is the Latinized version of the African Egyptian "Heru", which means "distant one above."

Compared to the bible in Christianity the most popular religion in the world today, Osiris would be the Father God, Horus would be the Son God, Isis would be the Virgin Mother and Ra would be the Holy Spirit.

Osiris is the one, the God, the Father, born from Ra, the spirit, who once lived as a human being upon the earth. His life on earth was perfect and the greatest. When Osiris grew up he married Isis. Osiris became sole ruler of African Egypt and was a good ruler, he was not feared. Osiris was the greatest, he taught the people knowledge, wisdom, religion, the art of agriculture, culture, truth and laws. Osiris was a good leader, he taught the people how to enjoy themselves with music and poetry and how to live peacefully and happily among each other. African Egypt was filled with peace during Osiris' rule. The opposite of Osiris is Seth. Seth is Osiris' sworn enemy. Seth is the evil one and who hated and envied Osiris. The more good Osiris did, and the more people loved and praised Osiris, and the happier mankind became, the more Seth hated Osiris and wanted to kill him. Seth was jealous, he envied Osiris and wanted to rule in his place.

Seth deceives and kills Osiris and takes over the land and then scatters his "body parts" of his spirit across African Egypt. The land suffers in Seth's rule. After Osiris' murder by Seth, Osiris became God of the Dead and was over the judgement of dead souls. In order to enter Osiris' kingdom, you had to be balanced and righteous. A person was not expected to be perfect. The dead had to take a certain journey where their heart was balanced against a feather of "Ma'at", which means truth, justice, righteousness or morality.

Osiris' wife is Isis. Isis is the Goddess, the Mother of Horus, who once lived as a human being upon the earth and who lived a great and good life. Isis was a good wife, mother and caregiver. Isis knew the secret name of Ra, the spirit, which gave her power also. She is known as the Goddess of love, marriage, fertility, children, health, medicine and wisdom.

After Seth deceived and killed her husband Osiris and took over the land, and scattered "body parts" of his spirit across Egypt, Isis slowly, piece by piece recovered the "body parts" of the spirit of Osiris and reconstructed his spirit. When the spirit was reconstructed, the spirit of Osiris came and impregnated his virgin wife Isis and nine months later the virgin Isis gave birth to her son Horus on December 25, the day we celebrate Christmas now.

Horus is the living God, son of Osiris the God of the dead and son of the virgin Isis. Horus is known as the sky God, which is connected with the Sun and the Moon. Horus is known as the distant one, the one brought forth from Ra, the spirit, bringing transformation. Horus is the avenger of wrongs and the defender of order.

One-day Osiris said to Horus in spirit, "Tell me what is the noblest thing that a man can do?"

And Horus answered, "To avenge his Father and Mother for the evil done to them."

This pleased Osiris and then he further asked, "And what animal is most useful for the avenger to take with him as he goes out to battle?"

Horus replied, "A lion would indeed be the best for a man who needed help, but a horse is best for pursuing a flying foe and cutting him off from escape."

Horus confronts Seth, claiming he has unlawfully taken the throne from Osiris, his father. Horus and Seth battle it out and eventually Horus is victorious. Horus is then praised as the avenger of wrongs. Horus conquers Seth and restores order, righteousness and justice in the world. In his rule, Horus is praised as the defender of order. When Horus passes from the earth, he comes back in spirit and Seth also came back in spirit and Horus and Seth battle for the souls of men and for the rule of the world. This fight between Horus and Seth is eternal.

The Ancient African Egyptians were mystical human beings, their religious beliefs developed and formed the concept of religion. Religion was very important to the Ancient African Egyptians, it was tradition and it influenced every aspect of their lives. The pharaohs in African Egypt were the political and religious leaders of all the people. The pharaohs considered themselves to be the Gods of the earth and held the title, "Lord of the Two Lands" and "High Priest of Every Temple". Of all the pharaohs who ruled Ancient African Egypt, the one who stands out from the rest is Akhenaten. Akhenaten was great, he ruled over Ancient African Egypt for 17 years and brought about a cultural and religious revolution that changed the world. Akhenaten was the anointed one, he was the first to introduce monotheistic worship, belief in one God.

Akhenaten worshipped the sun and proclaimed, "His God was not fashioned by human hands and that God's forms could not be known to a human being."

Akhenaten said, "Thy beams touch all he has created; thy beams appear, and all is nourished, and the land brightens at thy daily birth".

Akhenaten believed in self-enlightenment and stated, "the one who builds himself with his own hands, no craftsman, knows God." To receive understanding at the hands of others is to close the door of self-enlightenment. To know oneself at the deepest level is to know God.

CHAPTER 3

We Are Human Beings

A Human being is defined as the species Homo Sapiens. "Homo" comes from the Latin word "hominis", meaning "man", and the species name "sapiens", comes from the Latin, which means "Wise". The term "Homo Sapiens" literally translates to "Wise Man". Do you know what is the most important and main natural function of a human being is? It can't be just to simply grow because that would make us the same as a plant. It can't be just to simply see, feel, smell, hear, or taste because that would make us the same as a dog. What makes us different from animals, plants and unlike anything else in nature, is our ability to act with the power of the mind. Our brains are involved in every aspect of our lives, the way we can use our mind is what separates us from everything else in nature. Human beings are unique in nature.

You have a weapon, a very deadly one, an intellectual weapon, your mind. Be a master with your weapon, on point and accurate. Our mind is amazing, all human judgement, evaluation, comparison or reasoning is an interpretation of images, based on memory. The process of finding things "Good" or "Bad" is the work of your imagination. Human beings can organize their own mind and actions and premeditate.

Everything in nature is built with a purpose in mind. A human being just like everything else in nature. Everything is programmed to flourish in a certain way. A human being just like everything else in nature and uses the conditions around and available to flourish.

You are special, being born is a miracle, in each birth something new comes into the world, being the only one of its kind. All of us are different, this uniqueness is marked genetically in our DNA. Our exact genetic makeup has never occurred before and it will never be repeated. Our souls are a onetime wonder in this world. What we are is our body or job to some but who we are is expressed in our behaviors, words, and deeds.

We Are Human Beings

Human beings live with the limitation of their five senses and of their thought, we can only conceive reality as much as our human biology's allow us to do.

Young human beings can act from their own free will but do not make any real decisions that involve a lot of thought. Only adults, the mature or the conscious, have the faculties and mental power for complicated thinking and decision making. Human beings are capable of thinking and action so the unexpected should be expected. Human beings can do anything that is possible to do, we are able to conduct what is unlikely to happen, everyone is different and thinks differently.

Don't be so quick to judge a human being. You can't judge a human being's life by their ups and downs, judge a human being's life by the truths of right and wrong behaviors and by the truths of goodness or badness of human character that they have cultivated over time, developed and express.

We Are Human Beings

Who are you exactly? A human being is the choices they have made overall, the right and wrong behaviors they have expressed over time and the goodness or badness of human character they have cultivated and become.

Human behavior transcends us as individuals and cultures. People are diverse, there are people who try to make their ego something other than what it is and on the other hand there are people who become aware of their eternal identity. Each culture has its own unique patterns, which contain their own values and cannot be judged in the terms of the values of other cultures. Thoughts are culture related but what controls the thoughts about a certain culture is the whole social level of evolution. For example, if a black man asks, "How can white people live and love the way they are?" he applies black values. And if a white man asks, "How can black people live and love the way they are?" he applies white values. Everyone is different, and everyone has different values, value is the meaning that you choose to give it.

We Are Human Beings

The human soul is fascinating, and can be described and divided into three parts, thinking, spirit and desire. Thinking is the most important, it separates us from other animals in nature, it is the overseer of the soul and always seeks the best overall outcome. Thinking gives us the ability to make rational decisions and supply's the humans conscience. The human conscience is sent from God himself, it is the inner sense of what is right or wrong in a human's actions and motives. Spirit is everything, it is who you are. Spirit creates ambition, boldness, and readiness. Spirit also creates feelings like pride, anger and shame. The strong natural feeling of wanting something is the Desire. Desire is the basic, natural urges, like food, sleep and sex. A human being becomes balanced, when spirit and desire are not given free power but are shaped and guided by careful, rational thinking.

CHAPTER 4

Living in Two Worlds

The world is defined as the material universe, the natural features of the earth, and as everything that exist outside of oneself. Everyone knows of this world, but human beings live in two worlds. The definition of the world relates to the outer world, the outer world can be described as the forms of things that attract and get our attention from our eyes, the world of appearances, the world that we see, the projections of reality, and the external world. There is also an inner world, the world of things within themselves, an internal world, the world within reality, an eternal realm, a spiritual world, hidden from our view, a world of inner parts working together and forming the whole, deeper than the anatomy of a human being.

The way that we see the world is in three directions of measurement, length, width and height, this is the outer world. The outer world can be deceiving and seductive. Most people get mesmerized by a human being's appearances and don't see the psychology behind what they do or say. Some people will distort you one way and others will distort you another way, people are different. Human beings are basically a mixture of different, unique qualities and traits, common to our species.

Everything is constantly in motion. The world is in flux and nature is occurring in cycles, recurrent always, a never-ending process of living and dying, so the outer world has no eternal or permanent substance. Everything in the outer world either dies or changes form.

In the inner world, the way that we see the world is in a distinguishing way. We can see the world in a fourth direction, which is the perceiving of the outer world of appearances. The marvelous structure behind reality is the inner world. The inner world is spiritual, you can't see it with your eyes, it does not attract and get our attention like the outer world but our inner most being is the absolute truth.

The outer world is deceiving, people hide their inner truth. People appear in a certain way in the outer world, people have a persona they use in public that acts like a mask to distract others from the truth. The mask people wear falls off in the heat of the moment, finally revealing who people are through some type of action. The mask is a form of deception and protection, within what we see is the absolute truth.

To understand others, we must learn how to understand our own selves. Inner self knowledge is the key to understanding absolute truths which are universal and timeless. Absolute truth and knowledge is of a reality that exist on its own, independent, this type of truth and knowledge is unalterable truth. This type of knowledge is different from scientific knowledge. Scientific knowledge is not absolute, the whole history of science is a story of changing explanations and new explanations of old facts. Absolute truths, knowledge and wisdom are timeless, changeless and perfect. The inner world is permanent, timeless and eternal. Get to know your inner world and outer world to a degree in which you know yourself to be one with nature, and just in that degree a human being is nearer to awakening and self-enlightenment.

CHAPTER 5

Time and Space

Time is defined as the continued progress of existence and events in the past, present and future, as a whole. Space is defined as a continuous area available or occupied. Time and space are part of the outer world, they are appearances, so they have no real existence. Everything in the outer world is in time and space. Time and space appear with events. Where there is no event there is no need of time or of space.

Time was invented by human beings. Time was invented to explain growth, development, continuation, and change.

We exist in each moment between the clicking of the clock of time, each moment we are not quick enough to perceive. Space is the three-dimensional concept and time is the active counterpart. The laws of time and space are part of the outer world of appearances. Time does not really exist, it just seems to do so to us observers who put together a world of what we

Time and Space

see with the dimensions of time and space. There is no time in the inner world. Time and space are the way human beings perceive the world. Time has no real or independent reality.

The present is reality. The past is gone, and the future is a dream, all we ever have is the present moment. In time, the present does not exist. Time separates the past from the future. The present has no quality of time, the present is always and eternal. The process of cause and effect are dependent on time. The way human beings see the present is really the past, nothing is instantaneous, the present is already a memory by the time we have seized it. We can never make contact with the present by looking, feeling, smelling, listening, or tasting.

Time can be a good partner in discovery, in time we can see both our own nature and the nature of the world. Time itself is neutral, it can either be used destructively or constructively. The absolute truth of time is change. No one can stop change. Life is a series of cycles, wherever you are now it will pass. The nature of things is always moving, changing and evolving. Everything changes in time, consciousness

Time and Space

changes, children change, relationships change, beauty changes, health changes, strength changes, seasons change, and the list goes on. We are always moving in action with the given forces, always reacting with others through time and space. The forever changing nature of things is everywhere around you.

CHAPTER 6

Consciousness

Consciousness is defined as being awake and aware of the power of the mind itself and of the world. To be unconscious is considered to be sleep walking, unaware of the power of the mind itself and of the world. Are you conscious or unconscious? Consciousness is the essence of the inner world. All one really is, ever was, or ever will be is pure consciousness.

Consciousness is a form of energy that is always looking for an outlet. This energy is not only in the striving of human beings but is the life force of nature itself, it is in plants, in animals and in the inorganic world. Consciousness expresses itself as a kind of blind and purposeless sort of striving until it finds a purpose. For the average person consciousness keeps them working actively and constantly in line with what they are willing, there aim and their goals.

Science, history and philosophy are ways of saying how our consciousness has awakened and evolved over time. The modern world with all our technology is an example of our achievements as conscious human beings. Technology is one of human kinds great expression of consciousness and what it is capable of.

Consciousness expresses itself in many different forms, for example, Malcom X, Fred Hampton and Dr. Martin Luther King Jr. express their consciousness in politics. The absolute true story of human development is not about technology or scientific advancement but about the awareness of consciousness itself and the way it seeks expression. The unfolding of absolute truths and knowledge is the unfolding of the world and the unfolding of the world is the unfolding of consciousness. Everyone can be great in their own way according to what one loves and expects. Your human existence is about your passions, your self-interest, being only one way. It is freely chosen among others to realize and take interest in your passions.

Subconsciously we often stay with the inherited construction of ourselves and never make any advancement into contemporary progressive thinking that will help us survive in this highly technical and postindustrial age. The wisdom of our elders was great at a time, but progressive thinking and continual reassessment will help you avoid falling behind. Update your personal philosophy. Stagnation is the danger of traditional thinking.

Consciousness changes throughout our lives. As we age, we view the world differently. Some people are blind and unconscious, they are unable to see the real world for what it is. This blindness is not physical, and unconsciousness is not because of any outer or external force but because of their own inner, internal construction. Something that is perceived to be real can only happen if the age, maturity or consciousness allows it to be seen.

In consciousness, there is realization, realization is a matter of becoming conscious of that which is already realized. Realization is described as an act of becoming fully aware of something as fact. Part of realization is understanding that certain kind of language and communication that has nothing to do with what people are saying, you must look deeper, and this certain kind of language says a lot about a person's character.

CHAPTER 7

Reality

Reality is what you see and experience. Reality is unable to be changed. In reality the greatest part of whatever you do is careful observation and precise thinking. Everything that we see at every moment of our lives may not be the pure vision that we may have assume them to be. It takes consciousness, knowledge, wisdom, and discipline to see things as they really are, while with-holding personal judgement.

Wise people don't judge, they seek to understand.

By continually cycling between speculation, observation and experiments, we are able to see more and more aspects of hidden reality.

Carefully observe and see things for what they are. Focus in on your present circumstances and have intense realism. Accept reality for what it is, resist the feeling and temptation of wishing everything was different and embrace and accept your circumstances.

Pierce deeper and deeper into reality like a drill that penetrates a piece of wood through its motion.

The way that we see reality is by breaking down and splitting everything into parts, categories or divisions so we can fully understand them. The process of subdivision and classification goes on and on until you dig deep enough to get to the root, the absolute truth.

Finding the truth is like chopping down a huge tree with a lot of girth, you can't chop it down with one swing of your axe, you must continue to chip away at it and do not let up and eventually whether it wants to or not, it will fall over.

Human beings categorize everything. The hierarchy is the basic structure for all human knowledge and was invented by the Ancient African Egyptians, the hierarchy structure branches out and resembles a pyramid. The hierarchy is the basic human structure for all knowledge, kingdoms, empires, churches, businesses, armies, governments, scientific knowledge, technical knowledge, mechanical assemblies, computer software and the list goes on, almost everything is structured into hierarchies.

In reality there is no hierarchy, there cannot be a hierarchy in one whole, aspects may vary but the whole remains one. Cause and effect are two separate things in time but one whole thing in reality. Grow closer to the reality of nature itself and see the secrets that are invisible to most, the intuitive mind is a gift from God.

CHAPTER 8

Fearlessness

Fear is defined as an emotion caused by thinking and believing that someone or something is dangerous and someone or something might cause you pain. Fear can be described as a kind of prison that confines you within a limited range of action. Human beings experience two kinds of fear, physiological fear and psychological fear. Physiological fear that protects our survival, is not the same as psychological fear. Psychological fear is something we create with our own minds, when there is no danger to our survival. For example, you may have experience psychological fear the first time speaking or performing in front of a large number of people, this is completely different from physiological fear. Physiological fear is an instinct that protects our survival in actual or potential dangerous situations, it increases arousal and expectancy.

Fear can take over your mind if you let it. Human beings have the ability of forming concepts, this is a power which is sometimes abused. We must learn how to quiet the anxiety we feel whenever we are confronted with anything that seems overwhelming, complex or chaotic. Have a clear insight into the present circumstance and overcome the doubts and fears in your mind. Develop the habit of maintaining your cool and never overreacting. We must learn how to deal with all situations and cooperate with them in a relaxed manner, with grace. Combine relaxation with activity. Keep inwardly calm and clear even in the middle of violent chaos.

Knowledge is important to any form of action. Knowledge and preparation lessens your fear and protects you from danger. The less you fear the more power you will have. Fear causes, you to lose energy, momentum and confidence and that lowers your power.

What is it that you fear? We live our lives afraid of things, worrying about uncertainties, second guessing about thirdhand possibilities and when we actually encounter one of these fears it turns out to be something we can manage and learn from. Have a fearless approach to life, attacking everything with boldness, clarity and energy.

CHAPTER 9

Free Will

The essence of being a human being is having free will. Free will is defined as the ability to act from one's own freedom to decide what should be done in a situation, without limitation or restriction. What is it that you will to do? We are free to see and organize the world as we want to according to our own knowledge, wisdom and experience.

Things perceived are not the things as they are in the outer world but are in our own mind. A human being is built up by memories of all the reactions to their environment since birth. We don't have complete, full, free will. We think we have complete, full, free will because our minds give us this happy illusion.

What we have is a state of conscious thought. Decisions don't arise from consciousness, they appear in consciousness. You can do what you decide to do, but you cannot decide what you will decide to do. We don't decide the next thought we think of, thinking just happens on its own.

Free Will

We have no conscious control of our next thought. We don't know what we intend to do until intention arises. Where does our next thought come from? Our thoughts and our actions are the result of our own neurological wiring and our state of mind. Thoughts and intentions come from background causes. Our actions are often shaped by our unconscious wants. The more Awaken you are the more Free Will you have.

CHAPTER 10

Morals

You can look anywhere in the outer world, even through a microscope, every day, for the rest of your life and you will never find a single moral. Morals are part of the inner world. Morals are all in your head, they exist only in your imagination. Morals are defined as a person's standards of beliefs and behavior concerning with what is right and wrong. To understand what is good, you must understand the underlying methods to arrive at that good and to understand what is bad, you must understand the underlying methods to arrive at that bad. The understanding and appreciation of what is right and the behaviors of, is enough to make a person have right thoughts and the behaviors of.

There is a universal moral law and it is timeless and space less. The moral law is God given, the divine truth and is defined as an absolute principle defining the criteria of right action. Something unjust and wrong is out of harmony with the moral law.

Morals

Morals are extremely important, without morals the world becomes purposeless and valueless. We would live in a world where nothing is right, and nothing is wrong. Morals are more than just about what is right and what is wrong, morals define who you are as an individual. Without morals, everything just functions like machinery.

Question the morality of everything, rise as individuals from the bondage of half-truths and myths, and enter the clear, liberated and heavenly realm of absolute truth. Obey your inner spiritual truth, you have a moral responsibility to fulfill. The search for happiness must be seen within the deeper search for moral excellence.

CHAPTER 11

Good vs. Evil

The world is full of different people with different characters. Good is not good without evil and evil is not evil without good, just like you cannot love unless you hate, and you cannot hate unless you love. The ideal of everyone all together, different cultures, in a harmonious, compatible society, where everyone cooperates happily for the mutual good of all, without racism, jealousy, envy and greed, is not true, it is not possible, human nature won't allow it.

All throughout history there has been a battle between good and evil. The good demanding good qualities such as freedom, justice, equality and peace, and the evil demanding evil qualities such as unjust power, inequality, domination and control. Good is defined as morally right and evil is defined as immorally wrong. Are you good or evil? In a hierarchy of classification, the most important division is the first one, because this division dominates everything beneath it. If the first division is immorally wrong, you cannot build a good system from it.

Good vs. Evil

The test of the true is the good.

Good is not a social code or some intellectualized thought, good is direct everyday experience. We all have another side. We all have aggressive desires and a tendency to manipulate, we must learn how to recognize, balance, and control it. It all begins with inner peace of mind, listening to the inner truth. Inner peace of mind produces the inner truth and right values. Value is nothing but the meaning that you choose to give it. The right values produce the right thoughts. The right thoughts produce the right actions. The right actions produce a good human being.

Inner peace of mind has no direct relationship to outer circumstances. Inner peace of mind can come to a soldier in heavy combat. Inner peace of mind can give you a level of confident authenticity that naturally eliminates limitations.

You will encounter evil, there is too much in the world to avoid. Evil people are ruled by their selfishness, insecurities and ego. Evil opposes the truth. The evil one's are deceitful and are the messengers of the false. The evil one's put to shame that which remained in God's resemblance. The evil one's oppress the people and jail, exile and kill the messiahs. The evil made a fake imitation of the true God, leading people away from the truth. The good are hated and persecuted by evil and by the ignorant who think they are advancing the name of God but are unknowingly immorally wrong, not knowing who they really are.

A revolution does not only destroy a systematic oppressing government, it also destroys the systematic oppressing patterns of thought that created that government. Everything derives from the inner world, desire, pride, ambition, greed, egoism, all forms of selfishness. Everything you do is for yourself. If every human being lost the notion of selfishness, all the evils of the world would cease to exist. By not concentrating on yourself to a certain degree, life on earth would resemble the kingdom of heaven.

CHAPTER 12

Power

Power is described as authority and control. Power gives the orders, everyone wants power. For power evil acts are performed to preserve an individual ruler, culture or nation. People will do anything for power and when they get it, they will do anything to keep power.

All unarmed leaders, states and nations have been destroyed and all the armed leaders, states and nations have been victorious and in power.

What we see as normal today is deceiving and very misleading, because of power structures. Power should be only rightfully used but in reality, power is abused. The only reason for power to be rightfully used on any member of a civilized community, against their will, is to prevent harm to others. Only if a citizen's actions are demonstrably shown to be bad for others.

A government should not impose a law just because it is considered to be for the peoples own good. Laws and political language is used and abused to hide unjust actions. Government power is increased when more laws are enforced, and that means the people have less freedom. When power is in the wrong hands, and is enforced wrongfully it produces inequality. Inequality comes from the super wealthy and powerful. Inequality is unjust and wrong on every level. Inequality has highly negative consequences in a community and in the world as a whole.

CHAPTER 13

Pain

Pain is universal, inescapable and edifying. Pain hurts, and everyone experiences pain throughout life and it is different for everyone. There are diverse ways of feeling and describing pain. Each one of us has circumstances to overcome that evolve and transcend us.

Life in many ways is like a war. In a war there is pain, suffering, and death, and in the loss of a battle it gives the General the opportunity to see the reality and a strategy to better protect himself against the enemy later. For the individual, this suffering, pain or death can come private, publicly, personally or emotionally. Expect pain in one form or another. Understand the loss of a battle is not the loss of the war, a loss is a lesson, learn and prepare yourself for the next opportunity.

Almost every autobiography has a story with some sort of pain in it, telling how they learned their values from the pain.

Pain

Pain, mistakes and failures are different ways of learning, they tell you about your own inability to deal with a situation in the execution of the action.

See the good in pain. Pain is the negative face of the truth, it drives the process of evolution that takes place within an individual. Everyone deals with pain differently. Some people are filled with pain and insecurities and pass it on to others. It satisfies some people to tear other people down. The right thing to do is to absorb pain and use that energy constructively. Let pain fill you with energy and purpose. Make your pain count and let it fill you with power and take that energy out on what you love to do, everyone has a God given passion.

CHAPTER 14

Anger

The control of anger is a quality of a balanced and strong mind. Anger is defined as a strong feeling of aggression, displeasure, annoyance and hatred. What angers you? Don't be quick to anger, it captures our mind, closes off our perception of the world and stops full knowledge from arising. If you become angry and full of hate easily you are mentally weak. A mentally weak person acts from impulse and does not think first. Be patient when dealing with people. If you are quick to anger, one can be provoked to do an action or reaction. Anger solidifies a view of the other as an opposite and creates a conflict of win or lose.

Be victorious over your anger. A person with a strong mind, in control of themselves, thinks first then acts from careful reasoning and careful decision making. Use a contemplative approach in stressful situations, it provides room in your mind to see things in a natural, ordinary and original way. This victory over your anger embraces every aspect of life, rejecting any part of this victory over anger means that we have given up on the workability of the given situation. We don't have to relate on each issue or agree on every detail to respect each other. Learn how to control yourself and control your anger in any given situation.

CHAPTER 15

Happiness

Happiness is described as a feeling of pleasure and satisfaction. Happiness is the best feeling in the world. Happiness comes from what we think is good for us in the future. What makes you happy? When you have been constantly looked down upon, belittled and minimized in society you envy your oppressors, you become desperate to be seen as great, important and worthy of attention and that causes the wrong choice of wanting instant happiness. Instant happiness is temporary and easier than the more difficult job of turning around the effects of beings loss and finding your eternal self for real permanent happiness. Instead of looking for instant happiness your focus should be on finding and pursuing the life that is most full of meaning to you and happiness will naturally follow.

Everyone is different so everyone will have a different route to their happiness. Refuse to be handcuffed by the limitations of your upbringing, environment, or peers, and invest

Happiness

your energy directly into your goals. Real happiness comes from working on something important to us, being only one way, it comes from working on ourselves, working on our aims and working on our goals over time. Happiness is not pleasure but comes with that of a meaningful life. When we feel that we are acting to fulfill our highest function and purpose as a human being, inner happiness and peace naturally arises and shines within.

CHAPTER 16

Life and Death

One of the most important absolute truths about our life is that we will not be here very long. Everything that is born dies. We are all preordained to lose everything we ever had and everything we ever loved, including our own selves. There is wisdom in numbering our days and understanding the world is not our home forever. We all eventually meet at the funeral home. The average lifespan is around 27,000 days and we sleep a third of that time, so the days that we experience number less than 12,000 days.

What we will, what we want to do, and what we love to do is an expression of who we are, our character. Before you are born life is nothing, it is up to you to give it meaning. Life is manifestations expressed in a time-space context that creates experiences and memories. Life is the things that happen in this world and a person's personality reacts to life with a certain state of mind.

Life and Death

People like comfort, assurance and certainty but we live in an unpredictable, winner takes all kind of world. In life it is what we do not know that hinders us, it is always the unpredicted, unexpected or unanticipated that changes your world, both personal and public. The best situation can turn around and instantly become your worst crisis. Always contemplate and plan for the worst situation. Many of life's hardships get their power from unexpected timing, things that catch us off guard.

Everyday people die, eventually everyone dies but everyone does not agree about what death is. Science can't answer the question of, "Is there life after death?" Some people believe the inner self dies when the body dies, and other people believe their inner self will survive after the death of their bodies. The Great Ancient African Egyptians strongly believed in the afterlife, and if dualism is true and each human being has a soul and a body connected together, life after death is possible.

There are three things you can do about death, you can either desire it, fear it, or ignore it.

CHAPTER 17

Awaken

Each route to awakening is just as individual and unique as the person who is taking the journey but only those who come to realize that they have been living in ignorance, can discover the truth and free themselves and experience self-enlightenment. Whoever remains ignorant cannot experience self-enlightenment. Are you awake or sleep walking? Self-discovery involves inner turmoil. Inner self knowledge is the key to understanding universal truths.

A concept is something that someone may accept, and something someone may not accept, the truth is which no one can deny.

In normal reality every action is followed by its reaction, the same as every cause has its effect. The awakened thinks and lives above average, every action is not followed by a reaction and every cause does not have its effect. The awaken are free from constraint to react.

Awaken

If you are able to discover and understand oneself and bring forth what is within you, what you bring forth will save you. If you are distracted by the many illusions and do not bring forth what is within you, what you do not bring forth will destroy you. Once we have eliminated these false illusions in which we see, think, live and feel, the way will be visible towards self-enlightenment.

Darkness vanishes when light appears, just like ignorance vanishes when you come to have absolute knowledge.

The glory in being great is recognizing and understanding that you are not simply an animal with various urges for survival that can talk, you are not a machine without morals and principles, and you are not just a consumer with certain tastes and preferences, you are a knowledgeable, wise and awakened human being with individuality. Everyone experiences being asleep at the time of their ignorance, and when you come to have absolute knowledge it is as if you have been awakened. The more knowledge you acquire, the more awaken you become, the baptism of truth cleanses you. Awaken.

The Self-Enlightened

The Self-Enlightened lives less according to the blind urges of their Ego and are more in relation with the inner eternal world.

The Self-Enlightened thinks of and is conversant with what is right and the behaviors of.

The Self-Enlightened are satisfied and composed.

The Self-Enlightened have a dignified ease without pride.

The Self-Enlightened understands that what we do to others, we do to ourselves; the Self-Enlightened treat others how they want to be treated.

The Self-Enlightened

The Self Enlightened identifies with the formless spiritual substance, seeing themselves as a universal expression of nature.

The Self-Enlightened loves what is right and the behaviors of more than anything.

www.ingramcontent.com/pod-product-compliance
Lightning Source LLC
Chambersburg PA
CBHW020619300426
4113CB00007B/709